Name _____

READING
journal

Reading Journal & Tracker

Reading Journal & Tracker

BOOK REVIEW INDEX: Use these pages to list each book you read. The page number space is to record which page of the Reading Journal the corresponding Book Review can be found.

READING GOALS: Use the book graphics to write down some reading goals and color in the book covers when you've achieved your goals.

FINISHED BOOK STACK: Create a visual version of your finished book list by writing in the titles of the books you read and coloring them in accordingly.

BOOK WISHLIST & LIBRARY BOOKS: Use these list pages to jot down books you'd like to read or check out in the future.

YEARLY READING TRACKER: Visualize your daily reading habit, see how many days in a row you can read, or how many total days in a month/year.

BOOK BINGO: Fill in the chart with books you want to read, and mark off a space each time you finish one of the books. Treat yourself to a reading reward if you get a BINGO!

BOOK REVIEW: These pages are to be filled in as little or much as you would like. There are many options for ways to react and respond to your reading. Keep quotes, ask questions, share your thoughts, and even draw a little something.

schoolnest

ART + BOOKS + NATURE

www.theschoolnest.com

"In the case
of good
books, the
point is not to
see how many
of them you
can get
through, but
rather how
many can get
through to
you."

— Mortimer J. Adler

BOOK REVIEW INDEX

PAGE	BOOK TITLE	AUTHOR

PAGE	BOOK TITLE	AUTHOR

BOOK REVIEW INDEX

PAGE	BOOK TITLE	AUTHOR

READING

GOALS

10

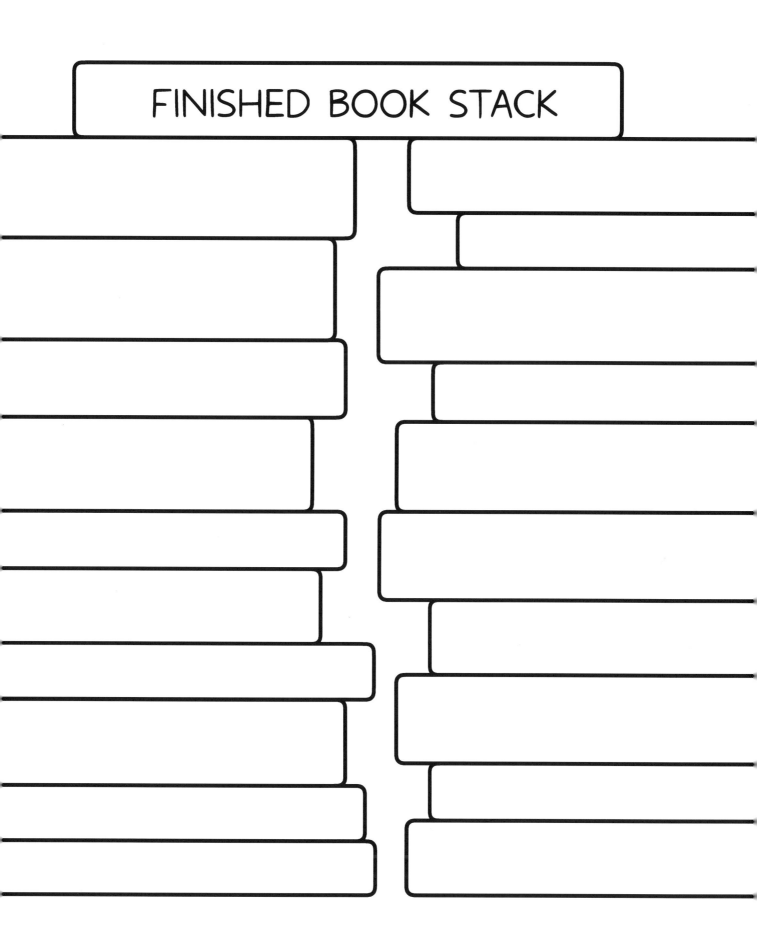

FINISHED BOOK STACK

FINISHED BOOK STACK

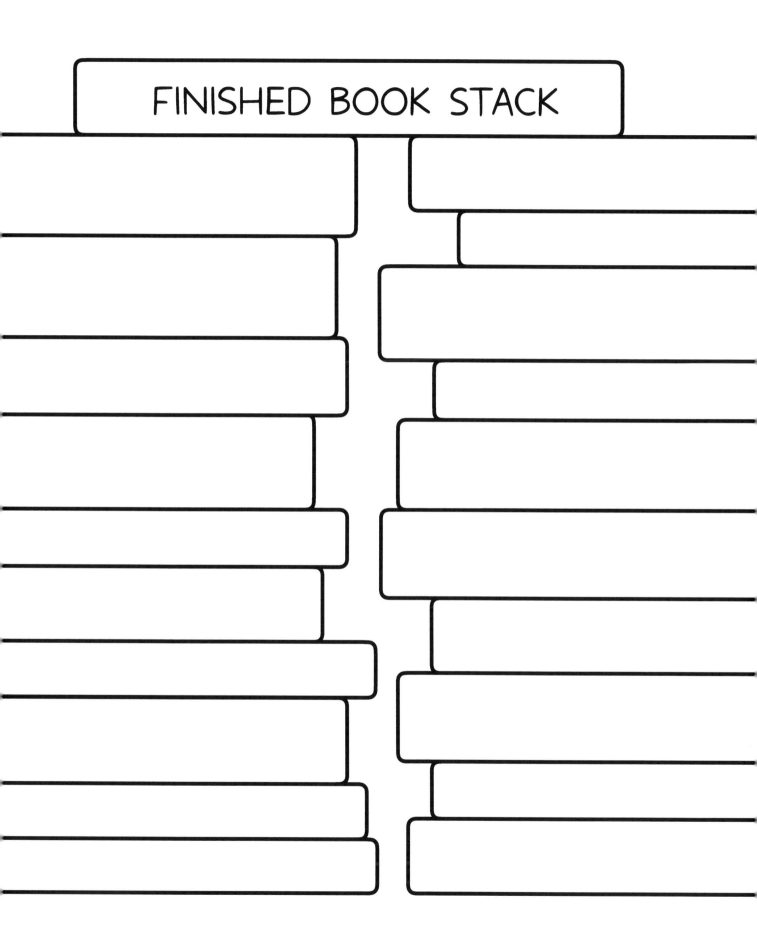

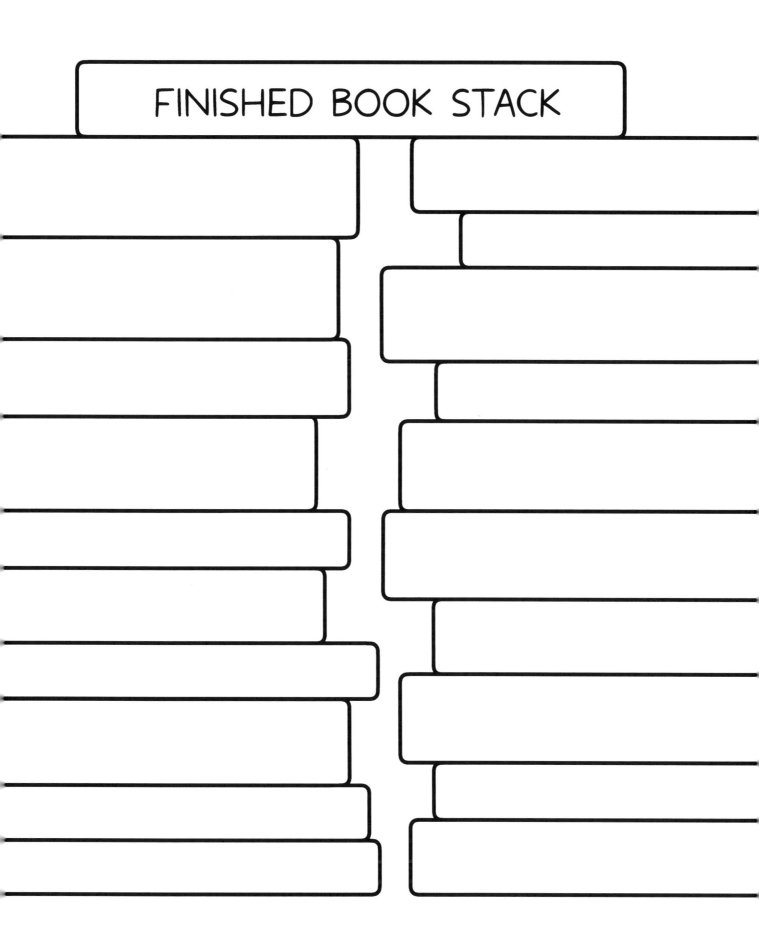

FINISHED BOOK STACK

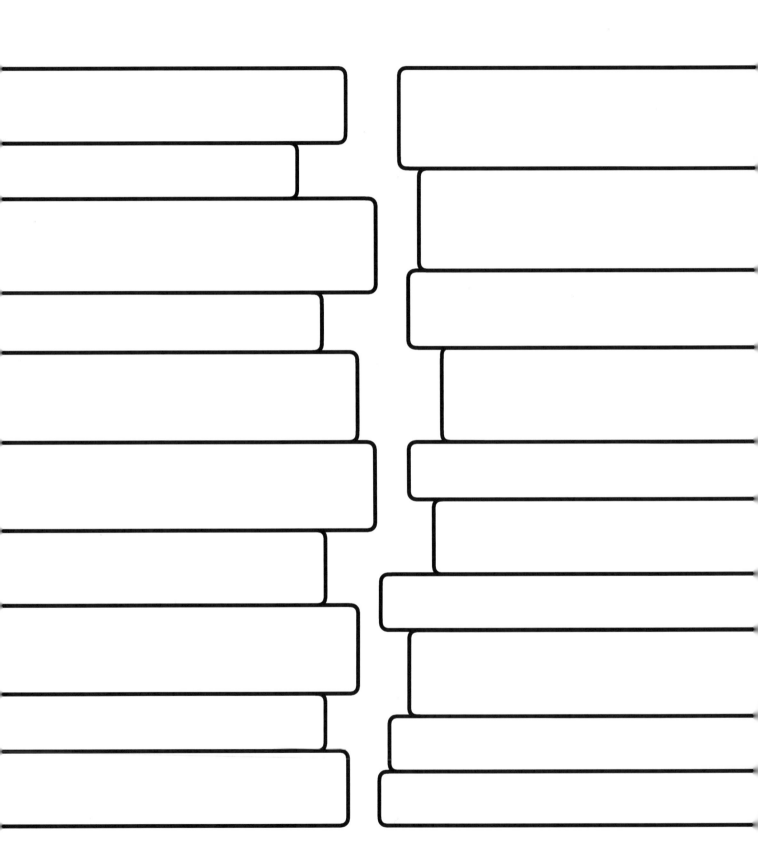

FINISHED BOOK STACK

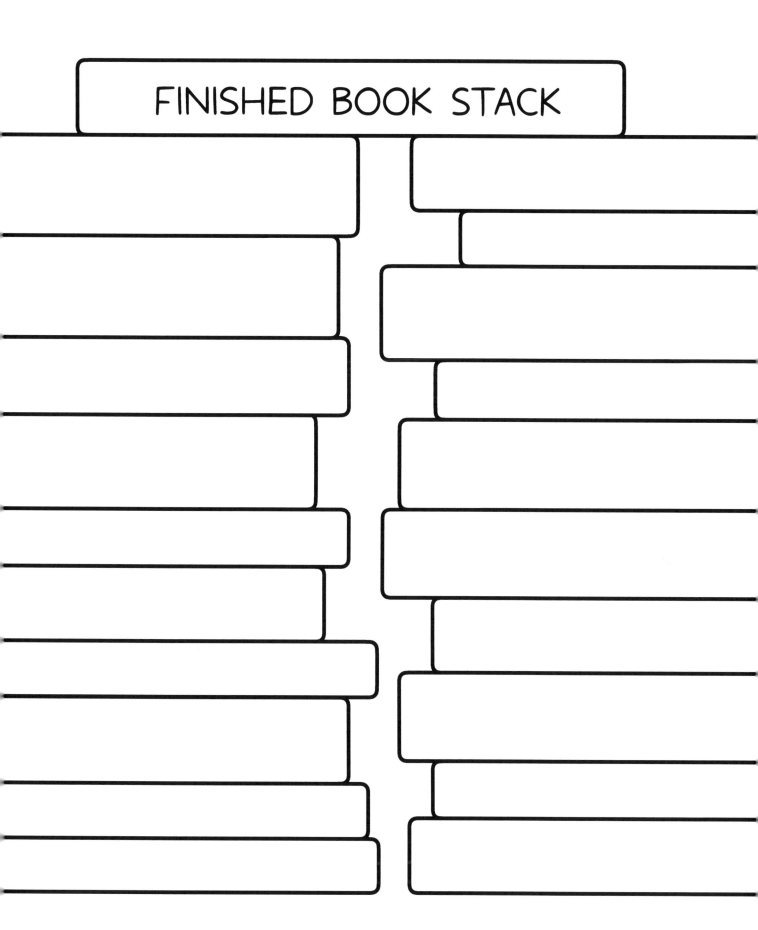

BOOK  WISHLIST

BOOK  WISHLIST

BOOK  WISHLIST

BOOK  WISHLIST

LIBRARY BOOKS

LIBRARY BOOKS

LIBRARY BOOKS

LIBRARY BOOKS

YEARLY READING TRACKER

month	1	2	3	4	5	6	7	8	9	10	11	12	13	14	15	16
	17	18	19	20	21	22	23	24	25	26	27	28	29	30	31	

month	1	2	3	4	5	6	7	8	9	10	11	12	13	14	15	16
	17	18	19	20	21	22	23	24	25	26	27	28	29	30	31	

month	1	2	3	4	5	6	7	8	9	10	11	12	13	14	15	16
	17	18	19	20	21	22	23	24	25	26	27	28	29	30	31	

month	1	2	3	4	5	6	7	8	9	10	11	12	13	14	15	16
	17	18	19	20	21	22	23	24	25	26	27	28	29	30	31	

month	1	2	3	4	5	6	7	8	9	10	11	12	13	14	15	16
	17	18	19	20	21	22	23	24	25	26	27	28	29	30	31	

month	1	2	3	4	5	6	7	8	9	10	11	12	13	14	15	16
	17	18	19	20	21	22	23	24	25	26	27	28	29	30	31	

month	1	2	3	4	5	6	7	8	9	10	11	12	13	14	15	16
	17	18	19	20	21	22	23	24	25	26	27	28	29	30	31	

month	1	2	3	4	5	6	7	8	9	10	11	12	13	14	15	16
	17	18	19	20	21	22	23	24	25	26	27	28	29	30	31	

month	1	2	3	4	5	6	7	8	9	10	11	12	13	14	15	16
	17	18	19	20	21	22	23	24	25	26	27	28	29	30	31	

month	1	2	3	4	5	6	7	8	9	10	11	12	13	14	15	16
	17	18	19	20	21	22	23	24	25	26	27	28	29	30	31	

month	1	2	3	4	5	6	7	8	9	10	11	12	13	14	15	16
	17	18	19	20	21	22	23	24	25	26	27	28	29	30	31	

month	1	2	3	4	5	6	7	8	9	10	11	12	13	14	15	16
	17	18	19	20	21	22	23	24	25	26	27	28	29	30	31	

month	1	2	3	4	5	6	7	8	9	10	11	12	13	14	15	16
	17	18	19	20	21	22	23	24	25	26	27	28	29	30	31	

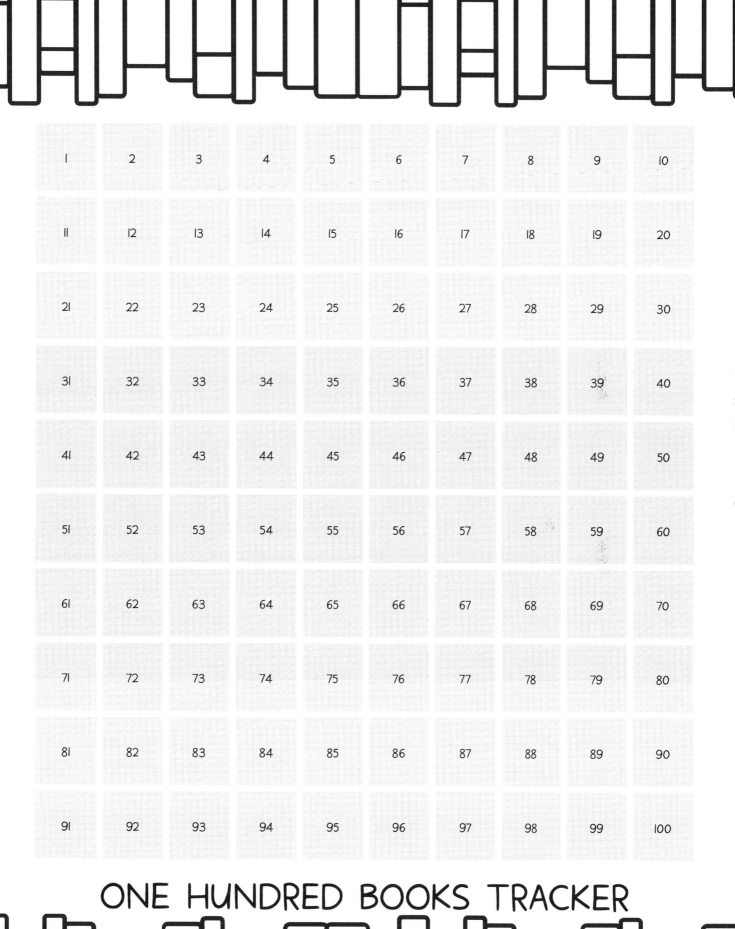

1	2	3	4	5	6	7	8	9	10
11	12	13	14	15	16	17	18	19	20
21	22	23	24	25	26	27	28	29	30
31	32	33	34	35	36	37	38	39	40
41	42	43	44	45	46	47	48	49	50
51	52	53	54	55	56	57	58	59	60
61	62	63	64	65	66	67	68	69	70
71	72	73	74	75	76	77	78	79	80
81	82	83	84	85	86	87	88	89	90
91	92	93	94	95	96	97	98	99	100

ONE HUNDRED BOOKS TRACKER

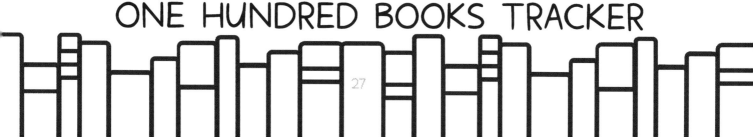

YEARLY READING TRACKER

month	1	2	3	4	5	6	7	8	9	10	11	12	13	14	15	16
	17	18	19	20	21	22	23	24	25	26	27	28	29	30	31	

month	1	2	3	4	5	6	7	8	9	10	11	12	13	14	15	16
	17	18	19	20	21	22	23	24	25	26	27	28	29	30	31	

month	1	2	3	4	5	6	7	8	9	10	11	12	13	14	15	16
	17	18	19	20	21	22	23	24	25	26	27	28	29	30	31	

month	1	2	3	4	5	6	7	8	9	10	11	12	13	14	15	16
	17	18	19	20	21	22	23	24	25	26	27	28	29	30	31	

month	1	2	3	4	5	6	7	8	9	10	11	12	13	14	15	16
	17	18	19	20	21	22	23	24	25	26	27	28	29	30	31	

month	1	2	3	4	5	6	7	8	9	10	11	12	13	14	15	16
	17	18	19	20	21	22	23	24	25	26	27	28	29	30	31	

month	1	2	3	4	5	6	7	8	9	10	11	12	13	14	15	16
	17	18	19	20	21	22	23	24	25	26	27	28	29	30	31	

month	1	2	3	4	5	6	7	8	9	10	11	12	13	14	15	16
	17	18	19	20	21	22	23	24	25	26	27	28	29	30	31	

month	1	2	3	4	5	6	7	8	9	10	11	12	13	14	15	16
	17	18	19	20	21	22	23	24	25	26	27	28	29	30	31	

month	1	2	3	4	5	6	7	8	9	10	11	12	13	14	15	16
	17	18	19	20	21	22	23	24	25	26	27	28	29	30	31	

month	1	2	3	4	5	6	7	8	9	10	11	12	13	14	15	16
	17	18	19	20	21	22	23	24	25	26	27	28	29	30	31	

month	1	2	3	4	5	6	7	8	9	10	11	12	13	14	15	16
	17	18	19	20	21	22	23	24	25	26	27	28	29	30	31	

? QUESTIONS

99 QUOTES

ILLUSTRATION

Book Review

TITLE

AUTHOR

DATE

RATING ★★★★★

📝 **SUMMARY**

💭 **THOUGHTS**

? QUESTIONS

99 QUOTES

 ILLUSTRATION

Book Review

TITLE

AUTHOR

DATE

RATING ⭐⭐⭐⭐⭐

SUMMARY

THOUGHTS

? QUESTIONS

99 QUOTES

 ILLUSTRATION

Book Review

TITLE

AUTHOR

DATE

RATING ★★★★★

📖 SUMMARY

💭 THOUGHTS

? QUESTIONS

99 QUOTES

 ILLUSTRATION

Book Review

TITLE

AUTHOR

DATE

RATING ⭐⭐⭐⭐⭐

SUMMARY

_____

_____

_____

_____

_____

THOUGHTS

_____

_____

_____

_____

_____

_____

_____

_____

_____

? QUESTIONS

99 QUOTES

ILLUSTRATION

Book Review

TITLE

AUTHOR

DATE

RATING ⭐⭐⭐⭐⭐

SUMMARY

THOUGHTS

? QUESTIONS

99 QUOTES

 ILLUSTRATION

Book Review

TITLE

AUTHOR

DATE

RATING ★★★★★

SUMMARY

THOUGHTS

QUESTIONS

QUOTES

ILLUSTRATION

Book Review

TITLE

AUTHOR

DATE

RATING ★★★★★

SUMMARY

THOUGHTS

QUESTIONS

QUOTES

 ILLUSTRATION

Book Review

TITLE

AUTHOR

DATE

RATING ⭐⭐⭐⭐⭐

SUMMARY

THOUGHTS

? QUESTIONS

99 QUOTES

✎ ILLUSTRATION

Book Review

TITLE

AUTHOR

DATE

RATING ⭐⭐⭐⭐⭐

SUMMARY

THOUGHTS

QUESTIONS

QUOTES

ILLUSTRATION

Book Review

TITLE

AUTHOR

DATE

RATING

SUMMARY

THOUGHTS

? QUESTIONS

99 QUOTES

ILLUSTRATION

Book Review

TITLE

AUTHOR

DATE

RATING ⭐⭐⭐⭐⭐

SUMMARY

THOUGHTS

❓ QUESTIONS

99 QUOTES

 ILLUSTRATION

Book Review

TITLE	AUTHOR

DATE	RATING ⭐⭐⭐⭐⭐

SUMMARY

THOUGHTS

? QUESTIONS

99 QUOTES

ILLUSTRATION

Book Review

TITLE

AUTHOR

DATE

RATING

SUMMARY

THOUGHTS

QUESTIONS

QUOTES

 ILLUSTRATION

Book Review

TITLE

AUTHOR

DATE

RATING

SUMMARY

THOUGHTS

? QUESTIONS

99 QUOTES

 ILLUSTRATION

Book Review

TITLE

AUTHOR

DATE

RATING ⭐⭐⭐⭐⭐

SUMMARY

THOUGHTS

? QUESTIONS

99 QUOTES

 ILLUSTRATION

Book Review

TITLE

AUTHOR

DATE

RATING ⭐⭐⭐⭐⭐

SUMMARY

THOUGHTS

? QUESTIONS

99 QUOTES

 ILLUSTRATION

Book Review

TITLE

AUTHOR

DATE

RATING ★★★★★

SUMMARY

THOUGHTS

? QUESTIONS

99 QUOTES

ILLUSTRATION

Book Review

TITLE

AUTHOR

DATE

RATING ⭐⭐⭐⭐⭐

SUMMARY

THOUGHTS

? QUESTIONS

99 QUOTES

 ILLUSTRATION

Book Review

TITLE

AUTHOR

DATE

RATING ⭐⭐⭐⭐⭐

SUMMARY

THOUGHTS

? QUESTIONS

99 QUOTES

 ILLUSTRATION

Book Review

TITLE

AUTHOR

DATE

RATING ★ ★ ★ ★ ★

SUMMARY

_____

_____

_____

_____

_____

THOUGHTS

_____

_____

_____

_____

_____

_____

_____

_____

_____

? QUESTIONS

99 QUOTES

ILLUSTRATION

Book Review

TITLE

AUTHOR

DATE

RATING ⭐⭐⭐⭐⭐

SUMMARY

THOUGHTS

? QUESTIONS

🗩 QUOTES

 ILLUSTRATION

Book Review

TITLE

AUTHOR

DATE

RATING ★★★★★

SUMMARY

THOUGHTS

99 QUOTES

ILLUSTRATION

Book Review

TITLE

AUTHOR

DATE

RATING ⭐⭐⭐⭐⭐

SUMMARY

_____

_____

_____

_____

_____

THOUGHTS

_____

_____

_____

_____

_____

_____

_____

_____

_____

? QUESTIONS

99 QUOTES

 ILLUSTRATION

Book Review

TITLE

AUTHOR

DATE

RATING ⭐⭐⭐⭐⭐

📖 SUMMARY

💭 THOUGHTS

? QUESTIONS

99 QUOTES

ILLUSTRATION

Book Review

TITLE

AUTHOR

DATE

RATING ⭐⭐⭐⭐⭐

SUMMARY

THOUGHTS

? QUESTIONS

99 QUOTES

ILLUSTRATION

Book Review

TITLE

AUTHOR

DATE

RATING ☆☆☆☆☆

📖 SUMMARY

_____

_____

_____

_____

_____

💭 THOUGHTS

_____

_____

_____

_____

_____

_____

_____

_____

_____

? QUESTIONS

99 QUOTES

ILLUSTRATION

Book Review

TITLE

AUTHOR

DATE

RATING ⭐⭐⭐⭐⭐

SUMMARY

_____
_____
_____
_____
_____

THOUGHTS

_____
_____
_____
_____
_____
_____
_____
_____
_____

QUESTIONS

QUOTES

ILLUSTRATION

Book Review

TITLE

AUTHOR

DATE

RATING ☆☆☆☆☆

📝 SUMMARY

_____

_____

_____

_____

_____

💭 THOUGHTS

_____

_____

_____

_____

_____

_____

_____

_____

_____

? QUESTIONS

99 QUOTES

 ILLUSTRATION

Book Review

TITLE

AUTHOR

DATE

RATING ⭐⭐⭐⭐⭐

SUMMARY

_____

_____

_____

_____

_____

THOUGHTS

_____

_____

_____

_____

_____

_____

_____

_____

_____

? QUESTIONS

99 QUOTES

 ILLUSTRATION

Book Review

TITLE

AUTHOR

DATE

RATING ★★★★★

SUMMARY

THOUGHTS

QUOTES

ILLUSTRATION

Book Review

TITLE

AUTHOR

DATE

RATING ⭐⭐⭐⭐⭐

SUMMARY

THOUGHTS

? QUESTIONS

99 QUOTES

ILLUSTRATION

Book Review

TITLE

AUTHOR

DATE

RATING

SUMMARY

THOUGHTS

? QUESTIONS

99 QUOTES

 ILLUSTRATION

Book Review

TITLE

AUTHOR

DATE

RATING ⭐⭐⭐⭐⭐

✏️ SUMMARY

💭 THOUGHTS

QUESTIONS

QUOTES

ILLUSTRATION

Book Review

TITLE

AUTHOR

DATE

RATING ⭐⭐⭐⭐⭐

SUMMARY

THOUGHTS

? QUESTIONS

99 QUOTES

 ILLUSTRATION

Book Review

TITLE

AUTHOR

DATE

RATING ⭐⭐⭐⭐⭐

SUMMARY

THOUGHTS

QUESTIONS

QUOTES

 ILLUSTRATION

Book Review

TITLE

AUTHOR

DATE

RATING ☆ ☆ ☆ ☆ ☆

📖 **SUMMARY**

_____

_____

_____

_____

💭 **THOUGHTS**

_____

_____

_____

_____

_____

_____

_____

_____

QUESTIONS

QUOTES

ILLUSTRATION

Book Review

TITLE

AUTHOR

DATE

RATING ⭐⭐⭐⭐⭐

SUMMARY

THOUGHTS

? QUESTIONS

99 QUOTES

 ILLUSTRATION

Book Review

TITLE

AUTHOR

DATE

RATING ⭐⭐⭐⭐⭐

SUMMARY

THOUGHTS

? QUESTIONS

99 QUOTES

 ILLUSTRATION

Book Review

TITLE

AUTHOR

DATE

RATING ⭐⭐⭐⭐⭐

SUMMARY

THOUGHTS

? QUESTIONS

99 QUOTES

 ILLUSTRATION

Book Review

TITLE

AUTHOR

DATE

RATING ⭐⭐⭐⭐⭐

SUMMARY

THOUGHTS

? QUESTIONS

99 QUOTES

 ILLUSTRATION

Book Review

TITLE

AUTHOR

DATE

RATING ⭐⭐⭐⭐⭐

SUMMARY

THOUGHTS

? QUESTIONS

99 QUOTES

 ILLUSTRATION

Book Review

TITLE

AUTHOR

DATE

RATING ⭐⭐⭐⭐⭐

SUMMARY

THOUGHTS

? QUESTIONS

99 QUOTES

 ILLUSTRATION

Book Review

TITLE

AUTHOR

DATE

RATING ⭐⭐⭐⭐⭐

📖 SUMMARY

💭 THOUGHTS

? QUESTIONS

99 QUOTES

ILLUSTRATION

Book Review

TITLE

AUTHOR

DATE

RATING ★★★★★

SUMMARY

THOUGHTS

? QUESTIONS

99 QUOTES

 ILLUSTRATION

Book Review

TITLE

AUTHOR

DATE

RATING ★★★★★

SUMMARY

THOUGHTS

QUESTIONS

QUOTES

ILLUSTRATION

Book Review

TITLE

AUTHOR

DATE

RATING ⭐⭐⭐⭐⭐

SUMMARY

THOUGHTS

? QUESTIONS

99 QUOTES

ILLUSTRATION

Book Review

TITLE

AUTHOR

DATE

RATING ☆☆☆☆☆

SUMMARY

THOUGHTS

? QUESTIONS

99 QUOTES

 ILLUSTRATION

Book Review

TITLE

AUTHOR

DATE

RATING ⭐⭐⭐⭐⭐

📖 SUMMARY

_____
_____
_____
_____
_____

💭 THOUGHTS

_____
_____
_____
_____
_____
_____
_____
_____
_____

QUESTIONS

QUOTES

 ILLUSTRATION

Book Review

TITLE

AUTHOR

DATE

RATING ⭐⭐⭐⭐⭐

SUMMARY

THOUGHTS

? QUESTIONS

99 QUOTES

 ILLUSTRATION

Book Review

TITLE

AUTHOR

DATE

RATING ★★★★★

SUMMARY

THOUGHTS

? QUESTIONS

99 QUOTES

 ILLUSTRATION

Book Review

TITLE

AUTHOR

DATE

RATING ⭐⭐⭐⭐⭐

SUMMARY

THOUGHTS

? QUESTIONS

99 QUOTES

 ILLUSTRATION

Book Review

TITLE

AUTHOR

DATE

RATING ⭐⭐⭐⭐⭐

SUMMARY

THOUGHTS

? QUESTIONS

99 QUOTES

 ILLUSTRATION

Book Review

TITLE

AUTHOR

DATE

RATING ★★★★★

📖 SUMMARY

💭 THOUGHTS

QUESTIONS

QUOTES

 ILLUSTRATION

Book Review

TITLE

AUTHOR

DATE

RATING ☆☆☆☆☆

📝 SUMMARY

_____
_____
_____
_____
_____
_____

💭 THOUGHTS

_____
_____
_____
_____
_____
_____
_____
_____
_____
_____

QUESTIONS

QUOTES

ILLUSTRATION

Book Review

TITLE

AUTHOR

DATE

RATING ★★★★★

SUMMARY

_____
_____
_____
_____
_____

THOUGHTS

_____
_____
_____
_____
_____
_____
_____
_____
_____
_____

? QUESTIONS

99 QUOTES

 ILLUSTRATION

Book Review

TITLE

AUTHOR

DATE

RATING

SUMMARY

THOUGHTS

? QUESTIONS

 QUOTES

ILLUSTRATION

Book Review

TITLE

AUTHOR

DATE

RATING ★ ★ ★ ★ ★

SUMMARY

THOUGHTS

? QUESTIONS

99 QUOTES

ILLUSTRATION

Book Review

TITLE

AUTHOR

DATE

RATING ★★★★★

SUMMARY

THOUGHTS

QUESTIONS

QUOTES

ILLUSTRATION

Book Review

TITLE

AUTHOR

DATE

RATING

SUMMARY

THOUGHTS

QUESTIONS

QUOTES

ILLUSTRATION

Book Review

TITLE

AUTHOR

DATE

RATING ☆☆☆☆☆

📖 SUMMARY

_____

_____

_____

_____

_____

💭 THOUGHTS

_____

_____

_____

_____

_____

_____

_____

_____

_____

? QUESTIONS

99 QUOTES

ILLUSTRATION

Book Review

TITLE	AUTHOR

DATE	RATING ★★★★★

📖 SUMMARY

_____

_____

_____

_____

_____

💭 THOUGHTS

_____

_____

_____

_____

_____

_____

_____

_____

_____

QUESTIONS

QUOTES

ILLUSTRATION

Book Review

TITLE

AUTHOR

DATE

RATING ★★★★★

✎ SUMMARY

💭 THOUGHTS

? QUESTIONS

99 QUOTES

ILLUSTRATION

Book Review

TITLE

AUTHOR

DATE

RATING ⭐⭐⭐⭐⭐

SUMMARY

THOUGHTS

? QUESTIONS

99 QUOTES

✏️ ILLUSTRATION

Book Review

TITLE

AUTHOR

DATE

RATING ⭐⭐⭐⭐⭐

SUMMARY

THOUGHTS

QUESTIONS

QUOTES

 ILLUSTRATION

Book Review

TITLE

AUTHOR

DATE

RATING

SUMMARY

THOUGHTS

? QUESTIONS

99 QUOTES

 ILLUSTRATION

Book Review

TITLE

AUTHOR

DATE

RATING

SUMMARY

THOUGHTS

? QUESTIONS

99 QUOTES

 ILLUSTRATION

Book Review

TITLE

AUTHOR

DATE

RATING ⭐⭐⭐⭐⭐

SUMMARY

THOUGHTS

? QUESTIONS

99 QUOTES

ILLUSTRATION

Book Review

TITLE

AUTHOR

DATE

RATING ⭐⭐⭐⭐⭐

SUMMARY

THOUGHTS

? QUESTIONS

99 QUOTES

ILLUSTRATION

Book Review

TITLE

AUTHOR

DATE

RATING ⭐⭐⭐⭐⭐

SUMMARY

THOUGHTS

? QUESTIONS

99 QUOTES

 ILLUSTRATION

Book Review

TITLE

AUTHOR

DATE

RATING ⭐⭐⭐⭐⭐

📖 SUMMARY

💭 THOUGHTS

❓ QUESTIONS

🗨️ QUOTES

✏️ ILLUSTRATION

Book Review

TITLE

AUTHOR

DATE

RATING ☆☆☆☆☆

SUMMARY

THOUGHTS

? QUESTIONS

99 QUOTES

ILLUSTRATION

Book Review

TITLE

AUTHOR

DATE

RATING ☆☆☆☆☆

📖 SUMMARY

_____
_____
_____
_____
_____

💭 THOUGHTS

_____
_____
_____
_____
_____
_____
_____
_____
_____

? QUESTIONS

99 QUOTES

ILLUSTRATION

Book Review

TITLE

AUTHOR

DATE

RATING ⭐⭐⭐⭐⭐

SUMMARY

THOUGHTS

? QUESTIONS

99 QUOTES

✎ ILLUSTRATION

Book Review

TITLE

AUTHOR

DATE

RATING ⭐⭐⭐⭐⭐

SUMMARY

THOUGHTS

? QUESTIONS

99 QUOTES

ILLUSTRATION

Book Review

TITLE

AUTHOR

DATE

RATING ⭐⭐⭐⭐⭐

SUMMARY

THOUGHTS

QUESTIONS

QUOTES

ILLUSTRATION

Book Review

TITLE

AUTHOR

DATE

RATING ⭐⭐⭐⭐⭐

SUMMARY

THOUGHTS

? QUESTIONS

99 QUOTES

✏ ILLUSTRATION

Book Review

TITLE

AUTHOR

DATE

RATING ⭐⭐⭐⭐⭐

SUMMARY

THOUGHTS

QUESTIONS

QUOTES

ILLUSTRATION

Book Review

TITLE

AUTHOR

DATE

RATING ⭐⭐⭐⭐⭐

📖 SUMMARY

💭 THOUGHTS

? QUESTIONS

99 QUOTES

✎ ILLUSTRATION

Book Review

TITLE

AUTHOR

DATE

RATING ☆☆☆☆☆

SUMMARY

THOUGHTS

? QUESTIONS

99 QUOTES

 ILLUSTRATION

Book Review

TITLE

AUTHOR

DATE

RATING ⭐ ⭐ ⭐ ⭐ ⭐

SUMMARY

THOUGHTS

? QUESTIONS

99 QUOTES

✎ ILLUSTRATION

Book Review

TITLE

AUTHOR

DATE

RATING

SUMMARY

THOUGHTS

? QUESTIONS

99 QUOTES

 ILLUSTRATION

Book Review

TITLE

AUTHOR

DATE

RATING ⭐⭐⭐⭐⭐

📖 SUMMARY

💭 THOUGHTS

QUESTIONS

QUOTES

ILLUSTRATION

Book Review

TITLE

AUTHOR

DATE

RATING ⭐⭐⭐⭐⭐

SUMMARY

THOUGHTS

? QUESTIONS

99 QUOTES

ILLUSTRATION

Book Review

TITLE

AUTHOR

DATE

RATING ☆☆☆☆☆

SUMMARY

THOUGHTS

? QUESTIONS

99 QUOTES

ILLUSTRATION

Book Review

TITLE

AUTHOR

DATE

RATING ☆☆☆☆☆

SUMMARY

THOUGHTS

QUESTIONS

QUOTES

ILLUSTRATION

Book Review

TITLE

AUTHOR

DATE

RATING ⭐⭐⭐⭐⭐

SUMMARY

THOUGHTS

? QUESTIONS

99 QUOTES

ILLUSTRATION

Book Review

TITLE

AUTHOR

DATE

RATING ★ ★ ★ ★ ★

SUMMARY

THOUGHTS

QUESTIONS

QUOTES

 ILLUSTRATION

Book Review

TITLE

AUTHOR

DATE

RATING ⭐⭐⭐⭐⭐

📖 SUMMARY

💭 THOUGHTS

? QUESTIONS

99 QUOTES

 ILLUSTRATION

Book Review

TITLE

AUTHOR

DATE

RATING ⭐⭐⭐⭐⭐

SUMMARY

THOUGHTS

? QUESTIONS

99 QUOTES

 ILLUSTRATION

Book Review

TITLE

AUTHOR

DATE

RATING ⭐⭐⭐⭐⭐

SUMMARY

THOUGHTS

QUESTIONS

QUOTES

ILLUSTRATION

Book Review

TITLE

AUTHOR

DATE

RATING ☆☆☆☆☆

📖 SUMMARY

💭 THOUGHTS

? QUESTIONS

99 QUOTES

ILLUSTRATION

Book Review

TITLE

AUTHOR

DATE

RATING ⭐⭐⭐⭐⭐

📖 SUMMARY

_____
_____
_____
_____
_____

💭 THOUGHTS

_____
_____
_____
_____
_____
_____
_____
_____
_____
_____

QUESTIONS

QUOTES

ILLUSTRATION

Book Review

TITLE

AUTHOR

DATE

RATING ☆☆☆☆☆

✎ SUMMARY

_____

_____

_____

_____

_____

💭 THOUGHTS

_____

_____

_____

_____

_____

_____

_____

_____

_____

_____

? QUESTIONS

99 QUOTES

 ILLUSTRATION

Book Review

TITLE

AUTHOR

DATE

RATING

SUMMARY

THOUGHTS

? QUESTIONS

99 QUOTES

 ILLUSTRATION

Book Review

TITLE

AUTHOR

DATE

RATING ★★★★★

SUMMARY

THOUGHTS

? QUESTIONS

〝〞 QUOTES

 ILLUSTRATION

Book Review

TITLE

AUTHOR

DATE

RATING ★★★★★

📖 SUMMARY

💭 THOUGHTS

? QUESTIONS

99 QUOTES

✏ ILLUSTRATION

Book Review

TITLE

AUTHOR

DATE

RATING ⭐⭐⭐⭐⭐

SUMMARY

THOUGHTS

? QUESTIONS

99 QUOTES

✎ ILLUSTRATION

Thank you for purchasing
a schoolnest notebook!

You can find a rainbow of notebook options
in many school subjects (math, spelling,
history timeline, science, grade level
composition books, journals, and more) on:

theschoolnest.com!

Follow along on Instagram @schoolnest

Made in United States
Orlando, FL
27 May 2022

18232861R00126